reaching ou

THE LUTHERANS

with heart
and mind

William J. Whalen

LIGUORI
PUBLICATIONS

One Liguori Drive
Liguori, Missouri 63057
(314) 464-2500

Imprimi Potest:
John F. Dowd, C.SS.R.
Provincial, St. Louis Province
Redemptorist Fathers

Imprimatur:
+ Edward J. O'Donnell
Vicar General, Archdiocese of St. Louis

ISBN 0-89243-206-3

Table of Contents

1. We've Come a Long Way

For many decades the Lutherans in the United States were isolated not only from Roman Catholics but from the rest of Protestant society as well. Many Lutheran congregations conducted worship in German or in a Scandinavian language, educated their children in parochial schools, avoided participation in interfaith agencies, and sat out Protestant crusades for Prohibition and Blue Laws. Protestants viewed their Lutheran neighbors as semi-Catholics who put crosses on their churches and followed a liturgy that looked suspiciously like the Catholic Mass. Many Catholics looked upon them as the destroyers of Christian unity.

All this has changed. Instead of keeping to themselves, the Lutherans have become aggressive evangelizers. Through radio and TV programs, information centers, and convert classes, they have brought their message to the American people. English has replaced other languages in the liturgy of almost all Lutheran congregations. Lutheran churches often set architectural standards in their communities. Lutheran music not only continues to secure their title as the "singing church" but "A

Mighty Fortress Is Our God" and other hymns of Luther resound in Catholic as well as Protestant churches. Today, few Christians, whether or not they embrace Luther's theology in every detail, deny his religious genius. One of the significant developments of the ecumenical movement has been the reevaluation of Luther by Roman Catholic scholars. Luther is now seen as a man motivated fundamentally by profound spiritual concerns.

American Catholics have, on their part, learned to respect the commitment of their Lutheran co-workers to the same Christian ideals of peace and justice; and in ever-increasing numbers are entering into the sacred union of matrimony with them, underscoring the need for further institutional reconciliation and also bringing a certain urgency into the matter.

This grass-roots outpouring of Christian love across sectarian barriers has made it essential that the average Catholic in the pew have a better understanding of his or her Lutheran brother or sister. Though recent studies have underlined the fact that individuals do not represent facsimile versions of the faith of their communities, each of us should try to understand the community vision and life that has formed a friend's or spouse's attitudes, aspirations, and expectations and continues to nurture his or her Christian growth.

2. *Parting Company*

THE LUTHERAN BREAK WITH ROME

The state of the Church, at the turn of the sixteenth century, was low. The man who has become known as probably the worst occupant of the throne of Peter — Alexander VI — reigned as pope during Luther's youth. To pay for the wars and luxuries of such popes, Rome continually sought new ways to raise funds. Clerical offices were bought and sold. The indulgence system became a gigantic scheme to funnel funds to the Vatican. The Renaissance popes often resembled Chinese warlords more than they did spiritual leaders. Many of the lower clergy lived in open concubinage while even the highest clergy sought favors for their illegitimate children.

The Man

Into such a world and such a Church was born Martin Luther (1483-1546), son of a peasant turned miner. Apparently, his upbringing was strict, and he suffered beatings at his father's hand. As Martin grew older, the family finances improved, and in 1496 Luther was sent from his hometown of Mansfeld to Magdeburg, where he attended a school operated by the Brethren of the Common Life. Five years later he entered the University of Erfurt, and in 1505 he began the study of law.

A dramatic incident changed his life. Martin was on his way to Erfurt when he was caught in a thunderstorm. A bolt of lightning threw him to the ground, and he made a vow on the spot that if he was spared he would enter a monastery. True to his vow, he joined the monastery of the Hermits of St. Augustine. Later he would write, "I regretted my vow, and many of my friends tried to persuade me not to enter the priory. . . . "

After only two years in the monastery Luther was ordained a priest, and in 1512 he received his doctorate in Scripture. Not only his intellectual but his administrative talents were recognized by his superiors, and he was assigned additional responsibilities.

The young friar threw himself into various ascetical practices. He spent as many as six hours trying to recall all his sins in the confessional. Once he went three days without even a crumb of food. He was barely able to finish his first Mass when he contemplated the power he had received to transform bread and wine into the Body and Blood of Christ.

At the new University of Wittenberg Luther underwent a period of intense religious torment. He continually asked himself, "What must I do to be saved?" His program of prayer, fasting, and penance failed to give him the sure answer he sought.

To find the answer, he turned to the Bible. Gradually, his new view of salvation took form. In his classes in 1515 and 1516 he concentrated on Saint Paul's Epistle to the Romans and was especially struck by the verse, "The just man shall live by faith" (Romans 1:17). Luther called this passage from the Bible "the gate of paradise."

In Luther's theology, man is by nature a sinner (the result of original sin), and his nature remains tainted by sin throughout his life. God bestows the free gift of his grace through faith. Man is saved not by his own efforts, by good works, but by faith alone. The justified man will perform good works, but these earn him no merit. "God alone. Faith alone. The Scriptures alone," declared Martin Luther.

Luther was repelled by elements of superstition and magic in the folk religion all around him. The Elector Frederick, who was also patron of the university, cherished his collection of relics which included a strand of Jesus' beard, a nail of the Cross, Saint Jerome's tooth, and a piece of the swaddling clothes! Those who viewed these treasures and offered a suitable contribution could obtain an indulgence of 1,902,202 years and 270 days.

The Incident

When Pope Julius II decided to build St. Peter's Basilica, he commissioned preachers to promote a new fund-raising indulgence. One of these preachers was a Dominican friar, Johann Tetzel, who began to offer this indulgence to people who lived near Wittenberg. The income from his efforts would be split between the Curia and the 24-year-old Archbishop of Mainz — after the banking house of Fugger had taken its share. Tetzel's methods were frankly commercial.

"As soon as the coin in the coffer rings, the soul from purgatory springs." Repentance was a minor element in the transaction; the money alone would guarantee that the donor or his friends and relatives would escape the punishments of purgatory.

Luther was outraged. He followed the usual procedure of his day by drawing up a list of theses or propositions for debate regarding indulgences and related topics. He posted his ninety-five theses on the church door at Wittenberg on October 31, 1517, and on the same day wrote the Archbishop of Mainz (not knowing the financial arrangement in which the prelate shared),

Papal indulgences for the building of St. Peter's are hawked about under your illustrious sanction. I am not denouncing the sermons of the preachers who advertise them, for I have not seen them, but I regret that the faithful have conceived some erroneous notions about them. These unhappy souls believe that if they buy a letter of pardon they are sure of their salvation; also that souls fly out of purgatory as soon as money is cast into the chest, in short that the grace conferred is so great that there is no sin whatever which cannot be absolved thereby, even if, as they say, taking an impossible example, a man should violate the mother of God. They also believe that indulgences free them from all guilt of sin.

Within a few months the theses were distributed throughout Europe, translated, debated, and called to the attention of the Roman authorities. At first the matter was dismissed by the Roman officials as just another monk's quarrel; they preferred their hunting and "politicking." But Luther's ideas were attracting too many adherents to be ignored and the Augustinian friar had also aroused the wrath of the powerful Dominican Order. The Dominicans controlled the apparatus of the Inquisition and also provided the personal theologian for the pope.

Although the immediate occasion for the posting of the ninety-five theses was the question of indulgences, Luther also considered such topics as the souls in purgatory, repentance, and the relative value of preaching the Gospel instead of advertising indulgences. Some of them were couched in provocative language. "Why doesn't the pope build the Basilica of St. Peter with his own money rather than with that of the poor, since he is wealthier today than the richest Croesus?"

When the reigning pontiff, Leo X, was elected pope in 1513, he is said to have remarked, "God has given us the papacy. Let us enjoy it." He no doubt would have preferred to forget about the disturbance in Germany, but the growing debate and pressure from the Dominicans forced him to act.

Nine months after issuing his challenge Luther heard from Rome. The papal document demanded that he report to Rome within sixty days to defend himself.

Because of the peculiar political circumstances of the time the young friar was able to defy the pope and insist on a hearing in his native Germany. To confront Luther the Vatican picked an able theologian, Cardinal Cajetan. The two met at Augsburg, but neither man understood the other. Luther refused to retract his words; he would agree to modify his positions, but only if he were shown that they were proved wrong by Scripture.

In the years 1519 and 1520 Luther devoted himself to writing. The breach with Rome widened as he attacked papal authority, expressed his admiration for the martyred Bohemian reformer Hus, and speculated that the institution of the papacy was perhaps the anti-Christ.

Rome demanded that Luther retract his errors in the ninety-five theses, but by now he had gone far beyond the positions he had advanced in 1517. Finally, on January 3, 1521, the pope excommunicated Luther and insisted that he be treated as an outlaw by both Church and state. When Luther received the papal bull he threw it on a bonfire while university students sang a *Te Deum*.

Called to defend himself before the Diet of Worms in 1521, Luther refused to renounce his writings and made a direct appeal to conscience,

> Unless I can be convinced by the testimony of the Scripture or by evident reason (for I believe neither the pope nor the councils since it is a fact that they have often failed and contradicted each other), I cannot and will not revoke anything. I am convinced by the texts of Scripture which I have quoted, and my conscience is held by God's words. It is neither safe nor fitting to act against one's conscience.

As a heretic Luther was considered an outlaw, but he was sheltered by friends. For a time he lived as "Junker George" in a castle at Wartburg while the Reformation moved ahead in Wittenberg. When Luther returned to Wittenberg in the guise of a bearded knight, he applauded most of the developments but objected to the destruction of statues and church art.

After Worms, Luther assumed less direction of the religious revolution he had started. Seven years after his original challenge to Rome he married a former Cistercian nun, Katherine von Bora; she bore him six children, and the couple also raised eleven orphans in their home.

In his remaining years Luther translated the Bible into German, prepared catechisms, revised the liturgy, wrote hymns, and preached. His most ardent admirers have been unable to approve everything he did. For example, critics have faulted Luther's approval of bigamy. Philip of Hesse, a Lutheran prince, tired of his wife and sought a divorce; but Luther objected. Luther proposed bigamy instead, on the grounds that the Old Testament countenanced plural marriage. He advised Philip to keep his second wife secret, but when the secret leaked out he suggested the prince resort to a "good and lusty lie."

In his old age Luther raged against the Jews, the papacy, and the sects. Plagued by constipation and insomnia, Luther nevertheless remained a gracious host and a good husband and father.

Lutheranism after Luther

Luther's associate, Philip Melanchthon, authored the Augsburg Confession (1530), which became the standard doctrinal statement of all the Lutheran Churches. In many ways it was a conciliatory document. For example, it states, "Confession in the churches is not abolished among us; for it is not usual to give the body of the Lord, except to them that have been previously examined and absolved" (Article XXV). It maintained that children should be baptized, that the Body and Blood of Christ are truly present in the sacrament, and that "the Mass is retained among us, and celebrated with the highest reverence." Yet, the Augsburg Confession also classified as "childish and needless works" such things as "particular holy days, particular fasts, brotherhoods, pilgrimages, services in honor of saints, the use of rosaries, monasticism, and such like." It insisted that "Scripture teaches not the invocation of the saints" and that priests be free to marry.

Various German princes abandoned Catholicism and cast their lot with the Lutherans. Lutheranism became the state Church of Denmark, Norway, Sweden, Finland, Iceland, Estonia, and Latvia.

Although the early Lutherans would have preferred that their new clergy be ordained by bishops, no Catholic bishops in Germany joined the Reformation movement. When the need to commission new ministers arose the Lutheran Churches decided that they would be ordained by the presbyters (priests or elders) rather than by bishops. In no circumstances did the Lutherans allow the lay members of a congregation to ordain their pastors.

Throughout its long history Lutheranism has produced giants in many fields of endeavor. To mention just a few: the composers Johann Sebastian Bach and George Frederick Handel; the artist Albrecht Dürer; philosophers such as Leibniz, Hegel, and Kant; the physician-scholar-missionary Albert Schweitzer; and the Nazi-era martyr Dietrich Bonhoeffer.

Today, the Lutheran World Federation reports a worldwide membership of about 70 million in 70 countries, the largest denomination in Protestantism. More than half of these Lutherans live in East and West Germany. There are also 7 million in Sweden, 4,300,000 in Denmark, 4,300,000 in Finland, and 3,200,000 in Norway. Lutherans in Asia and Africa number more than 3 million and those in Latin America exceed 900,000. About 750,000 Lutherans live in the Soviet Union in Estonia and Latvia.

3. Getting Reacquainted

LUTHERANS ON THE AMERICAN SCENE

The 9 million American Lutherans, mostly descendants of German, Swedish, Norwegian, Danish, Slovak, or Finnish immigrants, make up the fourth largest denomination in this country. Lutheran immigrants have been coming to America since the early seventeenth century.

Patterns of Immigration

The first such Lutheran settlers were Dutch merchants who arrived in New Amsterdam in 1624. A group of Swedish Lutherans established the colony of New Sweden along the Delaware in 1638. Pennsylvania welcomed many Germans, and by the middle of the eighteenth century more than 30,000 German Lutherans had made their homes in that colony.

Henry Melchior Muhlenberg, known as the patriarch of American Lutherans, did more than anyone else to bring together the scattered Lutherans in the colonies. In 1748 he organized the Ministerium of Pennsylvania, which embraced pastors and laity in four colonies.

A Lutheran helped win the first important victory for a free press in America. John Peter Zenger criticized the British administration in the pages of his *New York Weekly Journal*. He was jailed for sedition in 1735, but was freed by the jury after a powerful defense by his lawyer, Andrew Hamilton.

Lutherans came to America not only as Lutherans but as members of national churches; they wished to retain their own language, customs, etc. Between 1850 and 1860 almost 1 million Germans came to the U.S., and most were Lutherans. Immigration from the Scandinavian countries stepped up after 1870. Today, large Lutheran communities are found in Minnesota, Pennsylvania, Wisconsin, Illinois, and Michigan.

Not all these immigrants remained Lutherans, but those who did formed such bodies as the Augustana *Synod* (Swedish). ("Synod" is a term used to denote a mutually supportive union of Lutheran congregations, formed on an ethnic or geographical basis and confessing a common faith.)

The Desire for Unity and Orthodoxy

Over the years the scores of Lutheran synods have been consolidated through mergers into three major and a handful of minor groups. The major groups are: the Lutheran Church in America (the most liberal Church within this conservative tradition), the American Lutheran Church (the result of a 1961 merger of several Norwegian and German Lutheran Churches), and the Lutheran Church-Missouri Synod (torn at present by theological disputes and threats of schism).

In 1982, the delegates to conventions of the Lutheran Church in America, the American Lutheran Church, and the Association of Evangelical Lutheran Churches voted in principle, by large majorities, to form a united Church. The timetable calls for a convention to approve the constitution of the new body in 1987. With about 5,400,000 members the new Church will become the third largest Protestant body in the nation, after the Southern Baptist Convention and the United Methodist Church.

At the same conventions the three parties to the proposed merger approved an occasional interim sharing of Communion with the Episcopalians. The Episcopal Church passed a similar measure. Although not full intercommunion, the steps have been seen as an important ecumenical move.

The Lutheran theologian Martin E. Marty described the merger votes as a turning point that would move American Lutheranism from "creative foot-dragging to creative pacesetting." Archbishop John R. Roach of St. Paul-Minneapolis, president of the National Council of Catholic Bishops, called the decision of the Lutheran bodies to merge a "significant step in the broader movement of ecumenism." He added, "Roman Catholics join their Lutheran brothers and sisters in rejoicing at this new and important development."

After this merger 98.8 percent of Lutherans in the U.S. will belong to the new Church, the Missouri Synod, or the Wisconsin Synod. It appears that involvement of the Missouri or Wisconsin Lutherans in further Lutheran attempts at unity may be many years away.

The Missouri Synod

Until recent years, the Missouri Synod has shown great vitality and regularly won more converts than any other Lutheran Church. It has more congregations for the deaf than all Protestant denominations combined; its 1,000 grade and high schools enroll some 150,000 pupils. It also operates Valparaiso University, the largest Lutheran university in the United States.

In the early nineteenth century, a band of 700 Saxons sold their belongings and moved to St. Louis, Missouri, where they laid the foundations for the Church which became known as the Missouri Synod. These Missouri Lutherans viewed most other Lutherans in America with some suspicion. They considered these other Lutherans to be contaminated by rationalism and indifference to sound doctrine.

Their first leader was Pastor Martin Stephan. He persuaded the band to accord him the title "bishop" and assumed dictatorial powers; in time, however, he was accused of certain moral offenses and banished from the colony. The disheartened immigrants wondered whether the trip from Saxony had been wise.

Only the inspired leadership of young Pastor Carl F. W. Walther kept the group from disintegration.

Pastor Walther rallied the immigrants and was instrumental in the formation of the first organization of like-minded congregations. By the time of Walther's death in 1887, this Church had grown to 300,000 adherents in 24 states. Now the Missouri Synod reports 2,800,000 members and congregations in all 50 states, Canada, and a dozen Latin American countries.

The Missouri Synod accepts the Old and New Testaments as the Word of God and the Confessions of the Lutheran Church as the true and unadulterated exposition of this Word. Especially since the departure of many moderate seminary professors and pastors during the 1970s this Church has become more fundamentalist in its understanding of the Bible.

This branch of Lutheranism has stayed out of ecumenical bodies such as the National and World Councils of Churches. It would consider unity with other Lutheran Churches or other Christian bodies only after complete agreement in both doctrine and practice has been achieved.

A robust anti-Catholicism characterized many Missouri Synod publications until a couple of decades ago. Many older Missouri Lutherans were taught that the head of the largest Church in Christendom, the pope, was in reality the anti-Christ. This is still maintained by the smaller Wisconsin Synod, but Missouri and the other Lutheran Churches are now more likely to interpret Luther's view of the papacy as a historical judgment rather than an article of faith.

The Wisconsin Evangelical Lutheran Synod

Standing aloof from other Lutherans is the Wisconsin Evangelical Lutheran Synod, whose 407,000 members object to membership in the Boy Scouts, refuse to supply chaplains to the armed forces, view the doctrinal stands of other Lutherans with grave suspicion, oppose the teaching of evolution, and boycott the general Lutheran lay organizations. The Wisconsin Synod Lutherans once cooperated with the Missouri Synod in missionary and educational projects, but accused the Missouri Lutherans of liberalism and dissolved their alliance.

The Wisconsin Synod views the pope as the anti-Christ and generally rejects any ecumenical projects or cooperation with Catholics or other Protestants. Its more than 250 parochial grade schools enroll 30,000 pupils, and it also operates several high schools, two colleges, and a seminary. The Synod was founded in Milwaukee in 1850 and still counts half of its members in Wisconsin, but it also enrolls members in 47 other states and 13 foreign countries.

Always wary of any form of social activism, the Wisconsin Synod made a rare exception to its policy in 1979 when it overwhelmingly condemned abortion: "The unborn are persons in the sight of God and are under the protection of His commandments against murder." Members expressed grief "over the millions of the unborn who are being murdered each year through the willful sin of abortion."

The Smaller Lutheran Groups

Much smaller Lutheran groups are the Apostolic Lutheran Church of America (9,384 members), the Association of Free Lutheran Congregations (14,736), the Church of the Lutheran Brethren of America (10,423), the Church of the Lutheran Confession (9,426), and the Evangelical Lutheran Synod (19,885). These groups are composed of Lutherans of Scandinavian nationality or of those who level the charge of doctrinal liberalism at the larger Lutheran Churches.

4. Examining a Separate Tradition

LUTHERAN BELIEFS AND PRACTICES

All Lutherans accept the Apostles', Nicene, and Athanasian Creeds, as well as the Augsburg Confession and the Formula of Concord of 1580. To a non-Lutheran the theological differences among the major Lutheran synods are relatively minor. Lutherans do not allow the wide divergence of belief exhibited in, say, the Episcopal Church. In fact, Lutherans still hold heresy trials for pastors suspected of doctrinal aberration.

The Liturgy

The Lutheran liturgy has preserved much of the ritual, vestments, feast days, music, and prayers of the Catholic Church from which it broke away. At the same time, it embodies the special insights of the Reformation regarding the nature of man and his relationship to his Creator.

Luther's principle was expressed as an attempt to retain whatever was not expressly forbidden by the Scriptures; Calvin tried to purge the liturgy and the Church of everything which was not actually commanded by the Scriptures. As a result, Luther preserved far more of the Catholic heritage than did the Calvinists of France, Scotland, and Holland.

Calvinist churches were stripped of works of art. Ardent Calvinists smashed statues and stained glass in churches they commandeered. While Luther composed hymns for his Church, Calvin could scarcely conceal his antipathy toward music. Calvinists for centuries believed that only the Psalms were suitable for use in worship.

The whitewashed meetinghouse, not too dissimilar to a town hall, became the Calvinist architectural ideal. The Lutherans dispensed with side altars, but otherwise followed the traditional architectural pattern of the medieval Church.

Only in recent years have the Presbyterian and Reformed Churches turned to vestments, central altars in place of pulpits and organs, candles and flowers, stained glass and other art forms. These were aids to worship which continental Lutheranism never abandoned.

Lutheran immigrants to the United States continued to use their native languages in their liturgies for many decades. The unpopularity of German during the First World War induced many Lutheran parishes to de-emphasize German and add or expand English-language services. As the younger generation lost fluency in German and the Scandinavian languages and as converts joined the Church from other nationalities, German was relegated to perhaps one of two or three Sunday services. Parochial schools dropped German as the language of instruction, but some have retained it as a foreign language.

Luther retained a deep devotion to the Blessed Mother under the ancient title of the Mother of God. Roman Catholics ask her and the saints to intercede for them with God; Lutherans do not, but within the liturgical year in the Lutheran Churches certain days are set aside to commemorate the Blessed Virgin Mary, the apostles, the evangelists, the Church fathers, and other heroes of faith.

"The Supper of the Lord"

Luther tried to offer his followers a "reformed" Mass. The Augsburg Confession of 1530 states:

Falsely are our churches accused of abolishing the Mass; for the Mass is retained among us, and celebrated with the highest reverence. Nearly all the usual ceremonies are also preserved, save that the parts sung in Latin are interspersed here and there with German hymns, which have been added to teach the people (Article XXIV).

Luther expected his people to attend this Mass every Sunday, at which time Communion would be distributed under both species. The Augsburg Confession explained: " . . . we hold one communion every holy day, and, if any desire the Sacrament, also on other days, when it is given to such as ask for it."

For about 200 years after the Reformation this "Mass" remained the chief Sunday worship service in Lutheran Churches.

A Lutheran witnessing a Roman Catholic Mass would recognize most of the elements as similar to his own communion service. Likewise, a Catholic at a "high" Lutheran Church could recognize the extent to which the Lutheran liturgy has retained elements of the Roman.

Through the influences of pietism and rationalism the Lutheran Churches dropped the full "Mass" and used only the first part of the service on most Sundays. The full service, including the consecration and Communion, was held only once a month and on seven other days for a total of 19 times a year.

The Order of Morning Service without Communion ends after the Our Father with a Collect and Benediction. The Lutheran Church also prescribes rituals for Matins and Vespers, Baptism, burial, Matrimony, Confirmation, ordination, etc.

The trend toward more frequent celebrations of Holy Communion in Lutheran congregations has been evident in recent years. Fifty years ago some churches scheduled a communion service only once each quarter; now some Lutheran congregations hold a communion service every Sunday, and most would average about two such services a month.

The Real Presence

The Augsburg Confession states that Lutherans "teach that the Body and Blood of Christ are truly present, and are distributed to those who eat in the Supper of the Lord; and they reject those that teach otherwise."

Lutherans believe in the Real Presence but not in the Catholic doctrine of transubstantiation. Communicants believe that they are receiving the Body and Blood of Christ "in, with, and under" the bread and wine and are not simply memorializing the Last Supper.

A statement released by the Vatican Secretariat for Promoting Christian Unity and the Lutheran World Federation declared,

> Roman Catholics and Lutheran Christians together confess a real and true presence of the Lord in the Eucharist. . . . There are differences, however, in theological statements on the mode and therefore the duration of the real presence. . . . These two positions [on the mode of the presence] must no longer be regarded as divisive contradictions.

This 1978 document said both the Roman Catholic and Lutheran traditions "recognise that in the Lord's Supper Jesus Christ is present as the once-for-all sacrifice for the sins of the world. This sacrifice can be neither continued, nor repeated, nor replaced, nor complemented; but rather it can and should become effective ever anew in the midst of the congregation."

The Catholic parties to the joint statement did not authorize joint celebrations of the Eucharist but said that admission of Lutherans to Communion at Mass is possible "given sufficient reasons."

Baptism, Confirmation, and Confession

The other sacrament in the Lutheran tradition is Baptism, which is usually administered to infants.

Confirmation plays an important part in the life of the young Lutheran boy or girl entering adulthood, but it is not counted as a sacrament. Confirmation often is scheduled for Palm Sunday or Pentecost. The rite of Confirmation includes an examination on doctrine, a prayer by the congregation, and the laying on of hands by the pastor. As the pastor blesses each boy or girl he or she recites a verse from the Bible which carries a special meaning for the confirmed for the rest of his or her life. It is often incorporated into the individual's wedding service and funeral eulogy.

Luther continued the practice of private confession until his death, and his spiritual heirs may also avail themselves of this type of confession. The Reformer declared, "Without doubt confession of sins is necessary, and in accordance with the divine commandments." At another time he said, "The devil would have strangled me long ago, had I not this secret refuge of confession." He denied that confession should be compulsory and that the penitent can and should enumerate all sins.

The practice of confession was gradually abandoned during the seventeenth century, but has been revived in contemporary Lutheranism, especially in Germany. A public confession precedes each celebration of the Lord's Supper, but Lutherans can make appointments to confess privately to their pastors. Private confession in Lutheranism may be summarized: "None must; all may; some ought."

Marriage, Birth Control, and Abortion

Luther declared that marriage was not a sacrament but a civil contract. Lutherans uphold the permanence of the marriage bond, but allow divorce and remarriage in certain situations such as adultery and desertion.

All Lutheran synods now leave the question of birth control to the consciences of the married couples, although some pastors may privately frown on contraception.

The Missouri Synod recently called for a constitutional amendment outlawing abortions except when childbirth threatens the life of the mother. The church declared: "We as members of Christian congregations have the obligation to protest this heinous crime against the will of God, legally sanctioned in the United States and other lands." The statement added that "The practice of abortion, its promotion, and legal acceptance are destructive of the moral consciousness and character of the people of any nation."

"Orders," Authority, and Ministry

Lutheranism has never shown much interest in the validity or invalidity of priestly orders, although the Church of Sweden claims to have preserved the apostolic succession. In Luther's theology man stands in a direct relationship to God when he hears and accepts the Word of God. He does not need the mediation of a priest; as a Christian he belongs to the priesthood of the faithful.

Lutheran congregations choose their own pastors and govern their own affairs. They must, however, adhere to the doctrinal standards of the larger Church. Congregations send delegates to Church conventions which elect officers of the larger Church.

Until recently, none of the Lutheran bodies in the United States used the term "bishop," but preferred to call the elected regional and national officials "president." This has changed, but Lutherans do not attach the same meaning to the title as do Christians in the Roman Catholic, Eastern Orthodox, and Anglican traditions. Lutheran Churches in Europe have traditionally identified their leaders as bishops.

The role of deaconess was revived in Lutheranism in the early nineteenth century. These women, unmarried or widowed, staff hospitals and social service agencies. About 400 deaconesses serve in the various Lutheran bodies in the United States.

Lutheran Churches in Denmark, Sweden, and Slovakia have ordained women to the full ministry as have the Lutheran Church in America (LCA) and the American Lutheran Church (ALC).

5. *Moving Toward Reconciliation*

CONTEMPORARY LUTHERAN-CATHOLIC DIALOGUE

The Roman Catholic Church has been engaged in a number of ecumenical dialogues with representatives of other Churches since Vatican II, but probably no such dialogue has been more fruitful than that with the Lutherans. The U.S. Roman Catholic-Lutheran commission has published seven documents on theological topics such as the Eucharist, ministry, and, most recently, the question of justification. A similar international commission has produced five documents. In every instance the theological differences have been narrowed or even eliminated.

In 1983, the Lutheran-Roman Catholic Dialogue Group in the United States issued a joint statement on *Justification by Faith,* a crucial topic in the development of Lutheranism. For nearly six years the theologians in the group had examined their separate traditions with care and with a sympathetic ear to each other. The summary "Declaration," made at the close of that statement, indicates, perhaps better than anything else, the present climate of relationships between Roman Catholics and Lutherans in this country.

Thus we can make together, in fidelity to the gospel we share, the following declaration:

Shared Belief

We believe that God's creative graciousness is offered to us and to everyone for healing and reconciliation so that through the Word made flesh, Jesus Christ, "who was put to death for our transgressions and raised for our justification" (Romans 4:25), we are all called to pass from the alienation and oppression of sin to freedom and fellowship with God in the Holy Spirit. It is not through our own initiative that we respond to this call, but only through an undeserved gift which is granted and made known in faith, and which comes to fruition in our love of God and neighbor, as we are led by the Spirit in faith to bear witness to the divine gift in all aspects of our lives. This faith gives us hope for ourselves and for all humanity and gives us confidence that salvation in Christ will always be proclaimed as the gospel, the good news for which the world is searching.

This gospel frees us in God's sight from slavery to sin and self (Romans 6:6). We are willing to be judged by it in all our thoughts and actions, our philosophies and projects, our theologies and religious practices. Since there is no aspect of the Christian community or of its life in the world that is not challenged by this gospel, there is none that cannot be renewed or reformed in its light or by its power. (161, 162)

After this powerful statement of common belief, the group went on to make a sobering observation, to express its gratitude to God, and to offer a challenge to their Churches.

An Observation

We have encountered this gospel in our churches' sacraments and liturgies, in their preaching and teaching, in their doctrines and exhortations. Yet we also recognize that in both our churches the gospel has not always been proclaimed, that it has been blunted by reinterpretation, that it has been transformed by various means into self-satisfying systems of commands and prohibitions. (163)

An Expression of Gratitude

We are grateful at this time to be able to confess together what our Catholic and Lutheran ancestors tried to affirm as they responded in different ways to the biblical message of justification. A fundamental consensus on the gospel is necessary to give credibility to our previous agreed statements on baptism, on the eucharist and on forms of church authority. We believe that we have reached such a consensus. (164)

The European Background

The foundations for Roman Catholic-Lutheran dialogue were, of course, laid in Europe during the preceding decades. The Nazi experience and the forced mixture of Christian refugees after World War II in Germany contributed to the new understanding. Furthermore, a Council, Vatican II, that presented to the world a Church that saw itself as a "pilgrim" rather than as triumphant, and a pope, John XXIII, who spoke of the Church as "ever in need of reform" encouraged the hopeful. In the light of this new spirit, not only Martin Luther but the Reformation itself has been reevaluated.

The Basic Reevaluation

On the 450th anniversary of the presentation of the Augsburg Confession to Emperor Charles V as the bedrock exposition of Reformation principles, the joint Roman Catholic-Lutheran commission issued the following statement:

The express purpose of the Augsburg Confession is to bear witness to the faith of the one, holy, catholic and apostolic church. Its concern is not with peculiar doctrines nor indeed with the establishment of a new church but with the preservation and renewal of the Christian faith in its purity — in harmony with the ancient church and "the church of Rome," and in agreement with the witness of holy scripture.

The joint 1980 statement emphasized also that " . . . in content and structure, this confession, which is the basis and point of reference for other Lutheran confessional documents, reflects as no other confession the ecumenical purpose and catholic intention of the Reformation."

In a significant ecumenical gesture, Pope John Paul II became the first pope to worship in a Lutheran church. He accepted an invitation to participate in a joint service in a Lutheran church in Rome in 1983. The service included a prayer for Christian unity written by Luther. The pope took the occasion to declare: "On the 500th anniversary of the birth of Martin Luther, we seem to discern the dawning of an advent of recomposition of our unity and community." He added: "We desire unity, we work for unity, without letting ourselves get discouraged by the difficulty we encounter along our way."

6. Where Do You Go from Here?

As Lutheran and Roman Catholic theologians continue to report new successes in spanning the doctrinal rifts that separate their Churches, as more and more rank-and-file Christians of both denominations put aside the remaining vestiges of centuries-old mutual animosity, an ever-increasing number of Roman Catholic and Lutheran young people commit themselves to share a common Christian life in marital intimacy, regardless of painfully apparent institutionalized barriers still in place between their faith-support communities.

Such couples often find themselves at odds with the set policies of their Churches in the witness of their everyday lives or with the practices of their local officials. Sometimes, as a result of the ensuing battles, one or both spouses find themselves estranged from the communities through which the gift of faith came to them and through which it should be nourished.

What can such couples do? Contrary to the opinion of some, it is best that both members in such an interfaith union become more deeply involved with heart and mind in their respective Churches and more conversant with the wealth of their divergent traditions.

Such a practice need anticipate no conscience-disturbing compromise. It will rather give expression to a simple and humble admission that the development of faith of the Christians engaged in dialogue is in progress, and a consequent eagerness on the part of both to share with each other the growth in faith that each gratefully accepts as gift.

In this sharing, interfaith couples should find reassurance in the words of Bishop J. Francis Stafford to the world synod of Catholic Bishops in 1980, in which he referred to interfaith marriages as a "special opportunity for Christian growth."

He insists that such couples not be led "to ignore the real differences which exist in their faith orientation" but be encouraged to "search out and amplify areas of communality, truths on which they discover agreement and expressions of piety which bring both to a deeper awareness of God." The spokesman for the American bishops goes on to say, "What is behind this strategy is a belief in the authenticity of both faith orientations, if held in good conscience, and a hope that from their combination in the conjugal love, there will result a deeper marital union."

It goes without saying, of course, that if the non-Catholic partner feels called in his or her faith growth to join the Catholic Church, the Catholic partner will in no manner discourage him or her in this. This also is the intent of the Council fathers' respectful statement on *Religious Liberty* (3), "He is bound to follow this conscience faithfully in all his activity so that he may come to God, who is his last end. Therefore he must not be forced to act contrary to his conscience. Nor must he be prevented from acting according to his conscience, especially in religious matters."

We hope and pray that this booklet will help interfaith couples share the vision of faith. The absence of any kind of "discussion starters" is not an oversight; we felt that it would be presumptive, in matters so personal, to formulate the gifts that intimacy urges you to share.

Further Reading

Arnold, Duane W. H. and Fry, C. George, *The Way, the Truth, and the Life: An Introduction to Lutheran Christianity.* Grand Rapids, Michigan, Baker, 1982.

Bainton, Roland, *Here I Stand.* Nashville, Abingdon Press, 1950.

Bergendoff, Conrad, *The Church of the Lutheran Reformation.* St. Louis, Concordia, 1967.

Bodensieck, Julius, ed., *The Encyclopedia of the Lutheran Church.* Philadelphia, Fortress, 1965.

Edwards, Mark and Tavard, George, *Luther: A Reformer for the Churches.* Ramsey, New Jersey, Paulist Press, 1983.

Exploring the Faith We Share: A Discussion Guide for Lutherans and Roman Catholics. Ramsey, New Jersey, Paulist Press, 1980.

Lawless, Richard M., *When Love Unites the Church.* St. Meinrad, Indiana, Abbey Press, 1982.

Nelson, E. Clifford, *Lutheranism in North America: 1914-1970.* Minneapolis, Augsburg, 1972.

Todd, John M., *Luther: A Life.* New York, Crossroad, 1982.

Wentz, A. R., *A Basic History of Lutheranism in America.* rev. ed. Philadelphia, Muhlenberg Press, 1964.